Cushie and Friends

Cushie and Friends

A children's story with crochet patterns

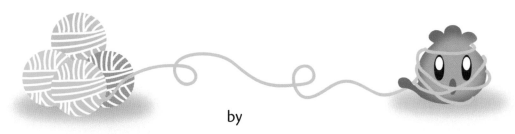

by

Jasmine Appelboom
story and idea

Sayjai Thawornsupacharoen
crochet patterns

illustrations: Maria K. Windayani

editor: Robert F.A. Appelboom

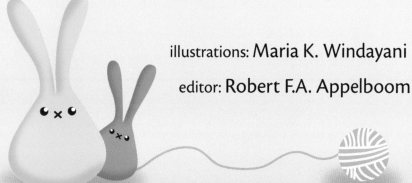

Second Edition
Sayjai's Amigurumi Crochet Patterns, volume 8

K AND J PUBLISHING
16 Whitegate Close, Swavesey, Cambridge CB24 4TT, England

Contents

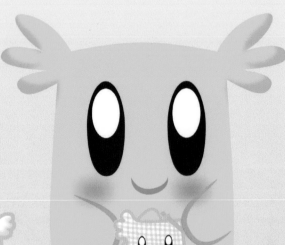

Introduction

Cushie and Cushionette are two sisters from Dream Island. They live in a wonderful world with their friends Jinco, Chickalee and Inky. But then, somebody steals all the dreamberries! What will happen to them?

You can create the beautiful dolls for Cushie, Cushionette and friends with the included crochet patterns. The patterns are written for beginners. The chapter "How to Crochet" teaches you all the crochet stitches to make the dolls, with step by step instructions and pictures.

We hope you'll love this story and wish you enjoyment and success creating the dolls.

Jasmine and Sayjai

Say hello to Cushie,

and Cushionette.

People say Cushie is the cutest in the land.

"No, I'm the cutest!"

"Of course
you are!"

They set off to find the lost dreamberries.

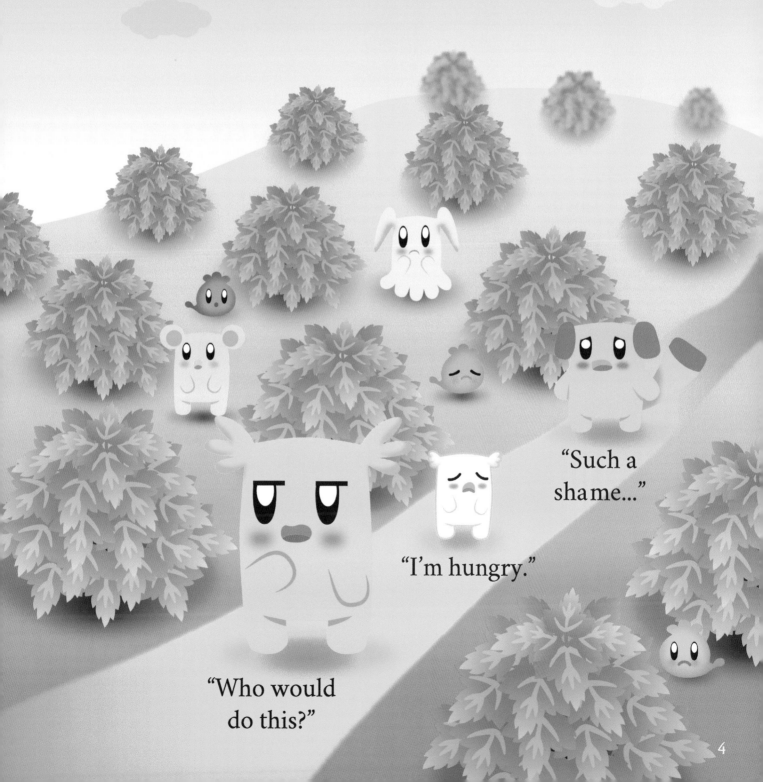

"Such a shame..."

"I'm hungry."

"Who would do this?"

4

They chatted with their friends Inky and Chickalee.
It turned out, Ooble had sneaked past with dreamberries.
They saw him go west.

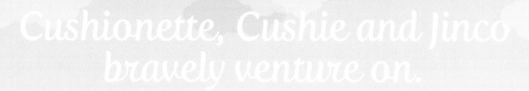

Cushionette, Cushie and Jinco
bravely venture on.

"I'm the queen of the
world!"

"Weee!"

"Oh, a trail."

They enter
the cave
and find...

Heaps of dreamberries.

Suddenly Ooble appears!

"Ha ha ha! You're far too late to stop me!"

"OH NO!"

"I'll trap you in this cave."

When just in time...
"Stop!
We won't let
you do this
to our friends"
"I catch you
with my licorice
ropes!"

"I'll throw ice cream!"
"Marshmallow attack!"
"Oh No! I do not like licorice."
"Me too."

Ooble is banished to a cave on Mount Avlove.

"Sigh"

And all the dreamberries returned.

How to Crochet

Before you start with the dolls, make sure you get the right hooks, yarn and stuffing. The materials are described on the next three pages: page 15 to 17.

The crochet stitches to make the dolls are shown step by step on the pages 18 to 25.

The chapter "Amigurumi Tips" describes techniques specific for making dolls, like "how to work in the round".

Gauge, doll size and abbreviations are explained on page 30.

The crochet patterns for the dolls are on the pages 31 to 60.

Materials

Hook

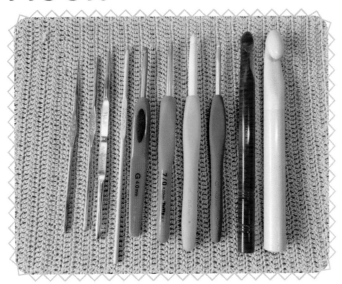

Crochet Hooks come in various materials and sizes, from a thin metal shaft to an ergonomic crochet hook. The thin metal shaft hooks are not expensive, but they are not comfortable.

They can give you cramp in your hand or even a blister, when you crochet a long time. I found the ergonomic crochet hooks much more comfortable than the metal hooks, because they have thicker handles. My favorite hooks so far are Tulip Etimo and Clover Soft Touch hooks.

You will be working at a very tight gauge* in Amigurumi projects. This can make you uncomfortable and you can easily get cramp in your hand. It is worth trying different hook types so you can find a hook which is comfortable and easy to use for you. Crochet hooks are a real personal preference, my preferred crochet hooks might not work for you. Many people prefer Clover Armour Hooks, but I do not like them. I found the handle too fat/ thick. Before you are committing to buy a full set of a particular brand, you should try them first.

* gauge = the number of stitches and rounds per inch

Crochet Hook Size Conversion

Hook in Metric (mm)	USA	UK	Japanese
1.00 mm	10 steel	4 steel	4 steel
1.25 mm	8 steel	3 steel	2 steel
1.50 mm	7 steel	2.5 steel	--
1.75 mm	4 steel	2 steel	--
2.00 mm	--	14	2/0
2.25 mm	B/1	13	3/0
2.50 mm	--	12	4/0
2.75 mm	C/2	--	--
3.00 mm	--	11	5/0
3.25 mm	D/3	10	--
3.50 mm	E/4	9	6/0
3.75 mm	F/5	--	--
4.00 mm	G/6	8	7/0
4.50 mm	7	7	7.5/0
5.00 mm	H/8	6	8/0
5.50 mm	I/9	5	--
6.00 mm	J/10	4	10/0
6.50 mm	K/10.5	3	7
7.00 mm	--	2	--
8.00 mm	L/11	0	8
9.00 mm	M/13	00	9
10.00 mm	N/15	000	10

Yarn

There are so many types of yarn : wool, acrylic, cotton, silk, synthetic, etc. If you are new to Amigurumi or crochet, acrylic yarn is the best to start with. It is economical, easy to find, does not stretch and is not slippery.

The stretchy yarn can easily make your work out of shape when stuffed tightly. The slippery yarn is difficult to work with for the beginner, because the stitches keep loosing up.

Yarn also comes in different thickness or weight. The Craft Yarn Council of America defined the Standard Yarn Weight System with 7 different size designations. Each size (or weight) is assigned a name, a number and recommended hook size.

Stuffing

I did research and found many types of stuffing: wool, cotton, corn fiber, bamboo fiber, polyester fiberfill, plastic pellets, glass pellets, etcetera.
I mainly use a good quality Polyester fiberfill and sometimes use Plastic pellets to add weight to a doll. These two are washable and keep their shape after a wash. They are inexpensive and easy to find.

Yarn Weight System

	USA	UK	AU	Recommended Hook in Metric (mm)
0 lace	Lace weight	1 ply	2 ply	1.5 - 2.25 mm
1 Super Fine	Fingering Sock	2 ply 3 ply	3 ply	2.25 - 3.5 mm
2 Fine	Sport	4 ply	5 ply	3.5 - 4.5 mm
3 Light	DK, Light worsted	DK	8 ply	4.5 - 5.5 mm
4 Medium	Worsted	Aran	10 ply	5.5 - 6.5 mm
5 Bulky	Bulky	Chunky	12 ply	6.5 - 9 mm
6 Super Bulky	Super Bulky	Super Chunky	14 ply	9 - 15 mm

Other Equipment

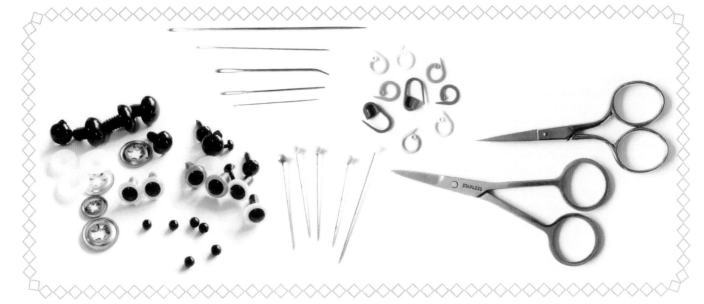

Needles

You can use a tapestry needle or needle with a big eyelet for sewing yarn. A normal sewing needle for attaching small beads, buttons or decoration pieces.

Stitch markers

A stitch marker marks the beginning of the round. You can use a safety pin or a piece of yarn instead of a stitch marker.

Pins

Pins are used for keeping ears, arms and feet in place.

Scissors

A small pair of pointed scissors is very useful to have when you are making a small doll. You can use the tip of the scissors to push the stuffing into a small part of the doll.

Eyes

Safety eyes have shafts on the back that you poke through the crocheted head. Then you attach a washer on the back. They have many sizes and colors.

You can also use buttons, beads or crocheted pieces for the eyes or embroider the eyes with embroidery thread or yarn.

Embroidery threads

Embroidery threads are used to embroider the eyes, eye lashes and mouth. They are sometimes used for crocheting small pieces.

Invisible thread

This is a clear nylon thread, used for attaching decorations and embellishments.

Craft glue

Glue is handy to have and used for attaching embellishments.

Other decorative items

You can decorate your dolls with ribbons, small buttons, beads, etcetera.

Crochet Stitches

This chapter shows you the crochet stitches used for the dolls. If you are new to crochet or have never made dolls before, then these photo series will help you to learn each stitch.

Tip: *On YouTube are very helpful videos which show how to learn all these crochet stitches.*

Slip Knot

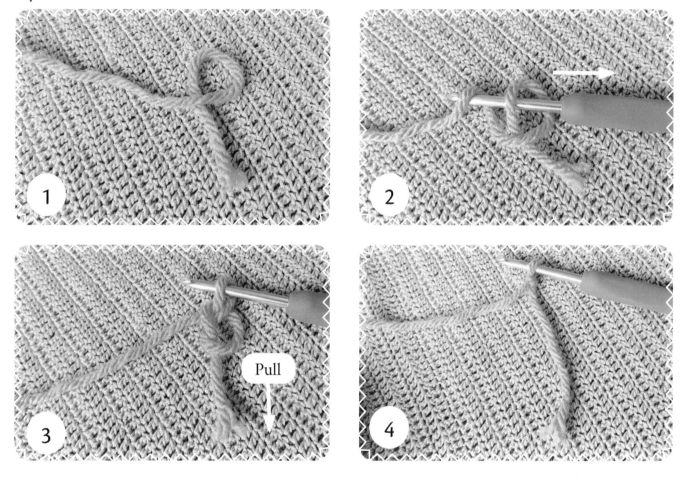

Chain Stitch (ch)

1) Yarn over the hook and pull it through the loop.
2) The first chain is made. Continue to work from (1) to create more chain stitches.

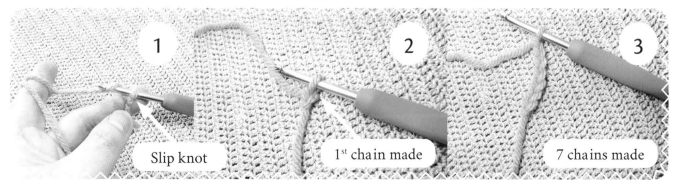

Slip knot | 1st chain made | 7 chains made

Single Crochet (sc)

1) Insert the hook into next stitch (or chain),
2) yarn over, pull yarn through the stitch (or chain).
3) You will have 2 loops on the hook,
4) yarn over and pull the yarn through both loops on the hook.
5) One single crochet (sc) is made.
6) Six single crochets are made.

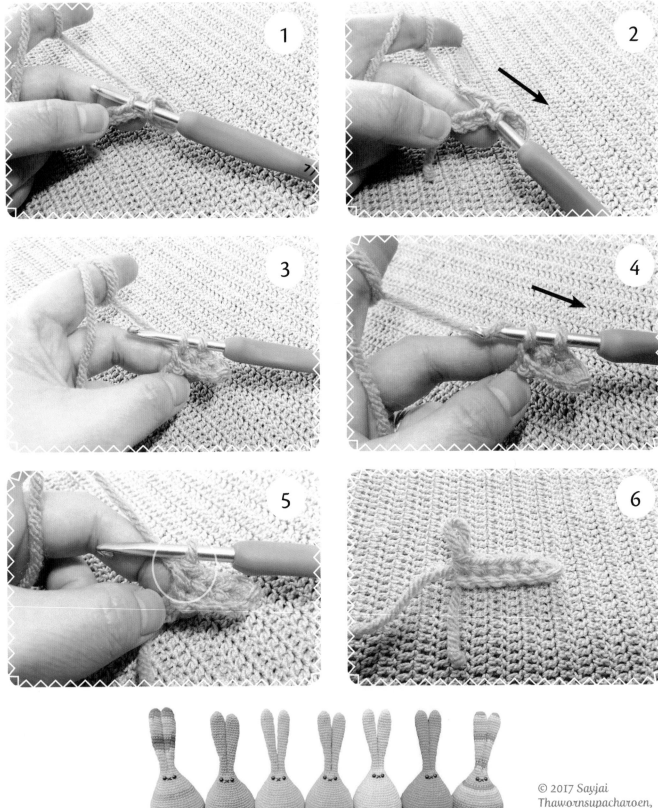

19

Half Double Crochet (hdc)

1) Yarn over,
2) insert the hook into next stitch (or chain), yarn over, pull yarn through the stitch (or chain).
3) You will have 3 loops on the hook, yarn over and pull the yarn through all 3 loops.
4) One half double crochet is made.

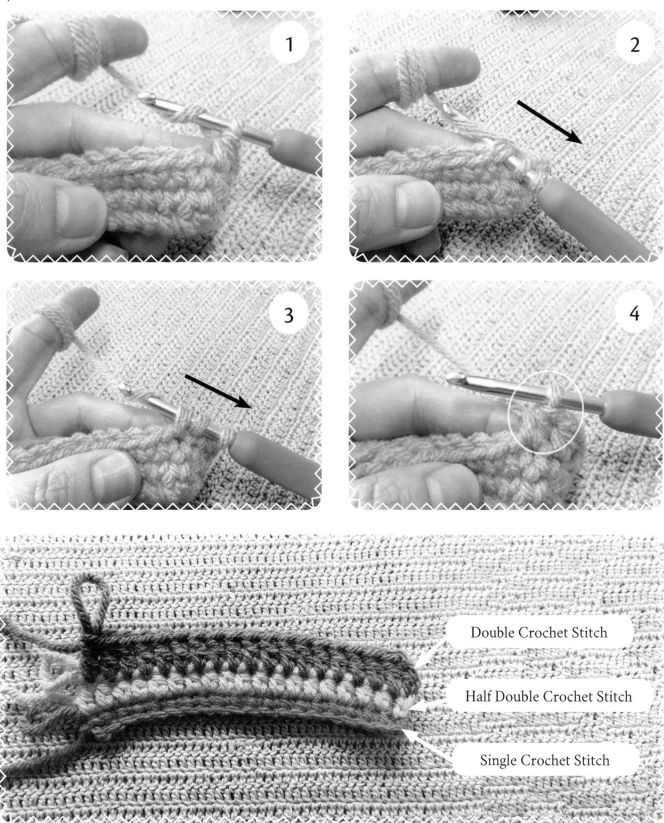

Double Crochet Stitch

Half Double Crochet Stitch

Single Crochet Stitch

Double Crochet (dc)

1) Yarn over,
2) insert the hook into next stitch (or chain), yarn over, pull yarn through the stitch (or chain).
3) You will have 3 loops on the hook, yarn over and pull the yarn through 2 loops on the hook.
4) You will have 2 loops on the hook, yarn over and pull the yarn through 2 loops on the hook.
5) One double crochet is made.

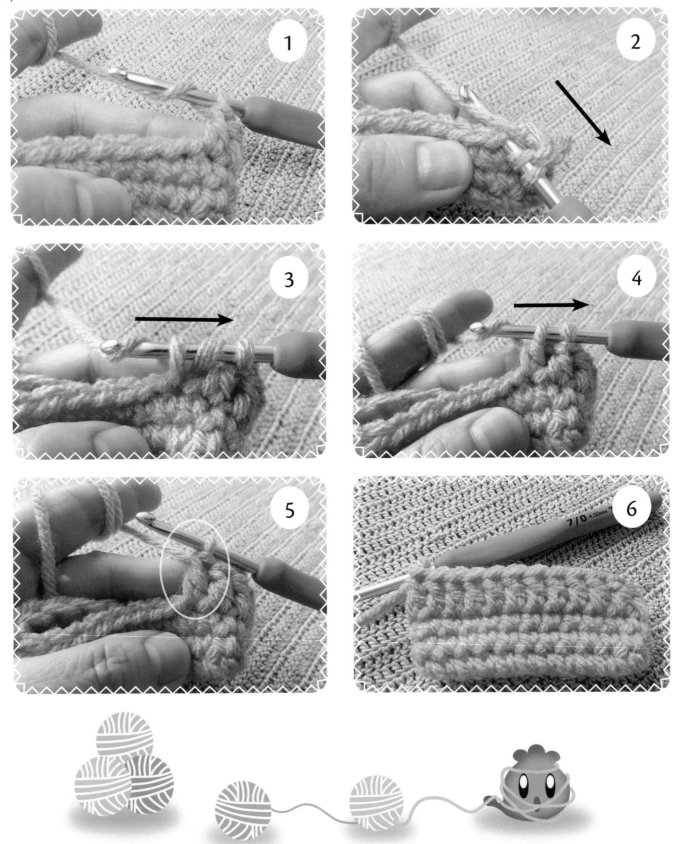

Working in Front or Back Loop

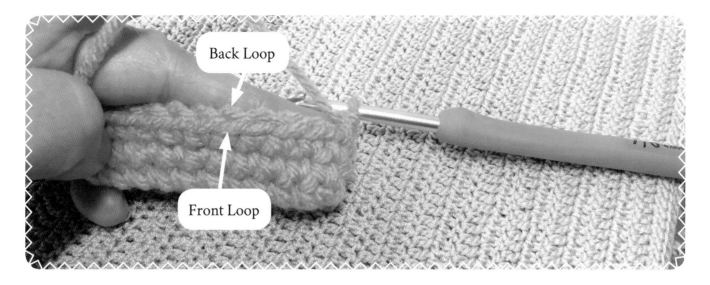

Back Loop

Front Loop

Working in Back Loop

To work in the back loop of a stitch, insert your hook underneath the back loop only and make the stitch as indicated in the pattern.

The pictures below show working single crochet in back loops only. You will see free loops in the front (right side).

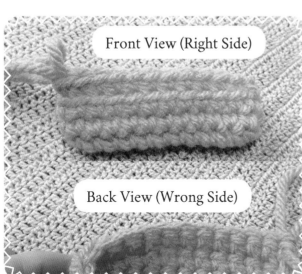

Front View (Right Side)

Back View (Wrong Side)

Working in Front Loop

To work in the front loop of a stitch, insert your hook underneath the front loop only and make the stitch as indicated in the pattern.

The pictures below show working single crochet in front loops only. You will see free loops in the back (wrong side).

Front View (Right Side)

Back View (Wrong Side)

Single Crochet Increase (2 single crochet in same stitch)

1) Insert the hook into next stitch (or chain), yarn over, pull yarn through the stitch (or chain).
2) You will have 2 loops on the hook, yarn over and pull the yarn through both loops on the hook,
3) the first sc is made.
4) Insert the hook into same stitch (or chain), yarn over, pull yarn through the stitch (or chain).
5) You will have 2 loops on the hook, yarn over and pull the yarn through both loops on the hook,
6) the second sc is made.

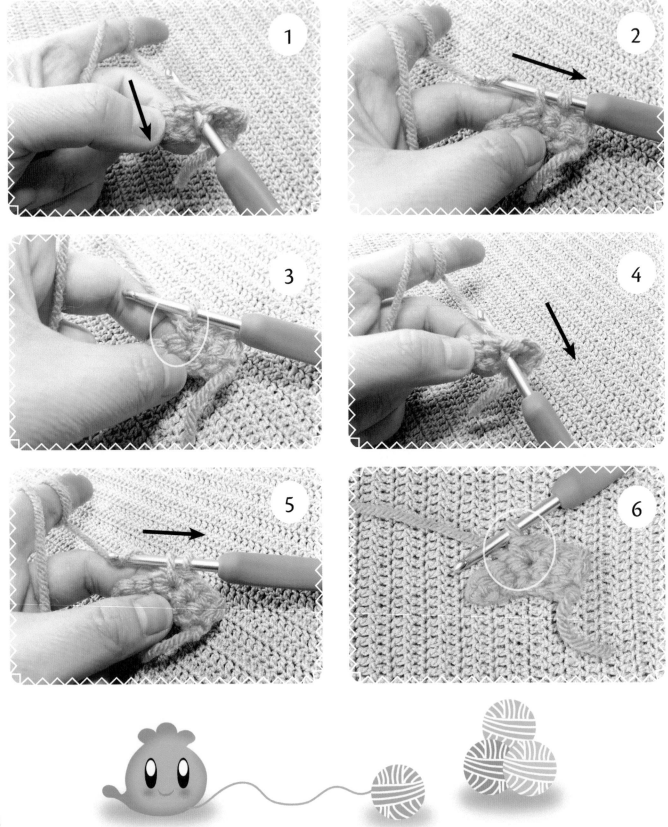

Single Crochet Decrease (single crochet next 2 stitches together)

1) Insert the hook into next stitch (or chain), yarn over, pull yarn through the stitch (or chain).
2) You will have 2 loops on the hook,
3) insert the hook into next stitch, yarn over and pull the yarn through the stitch.
4) You will have 3 loops on the hook,
5) yarn over the hook and pull through 3 loops on the hook.
6) Single crochet decrease made ("Sc next 2 sts tog").

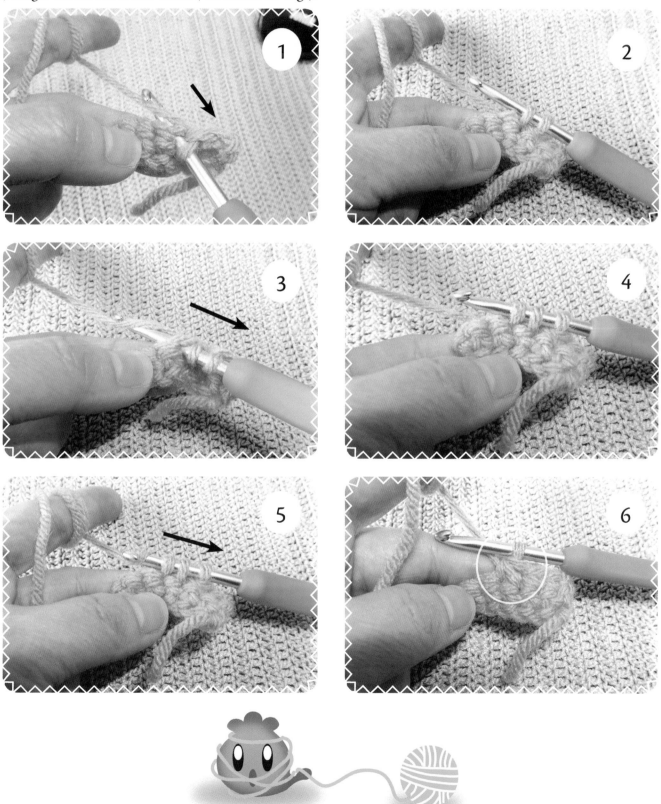

Slip Stitch (sl st)

1) Insert the hook into next stitch (or chain), yarn over and pull the yarn through the stitch (or chain) and a loop on the hook.
2) One slip stitch (sl st) is made.

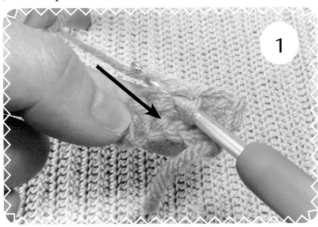

Fasten off

Cut the yarn about 1-2 inch long. If the pattern says "leave long end for sewing", leave the yarn long enough for sewing to the other piece. Put the yarn end through the loop and pull tight.

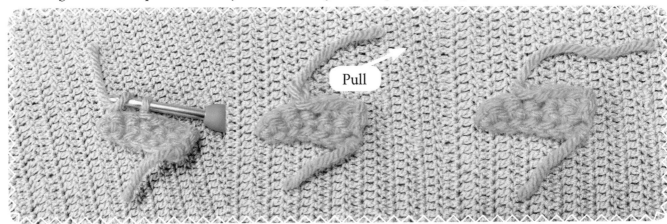

Pull

How to crochet 2 strands of yarn together

"Crochet 2 strands of yarn together" means holding 2 strands of yarn together when you crochet.

Amigurumi Tips

Foundation Magic Ring (Adjustable ring)

Begin with an adjustable ring (magic ring) and you will crochet the rows or rounds of your project on top of this ring. The finished piece will be a circle or spherical shape.

Basic Magic Ring

1) Put the yarn end behind the yarn from the ball/ skein to make a loop.
2) Put the hook through the loop and yarn over the hook. Pull the yarn through the loop.
3) The ring is made.

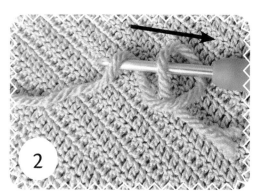

Continuous Rounds(Spirals)

Working in continuous rounds is when you come to the end of the round, you crochet into the first stitch of the previous round and keep going. It is useful to mark the first stitch of each round with a stitch marker or a piece of yarn. Because it will be difficult to identify where the round begins or ends.

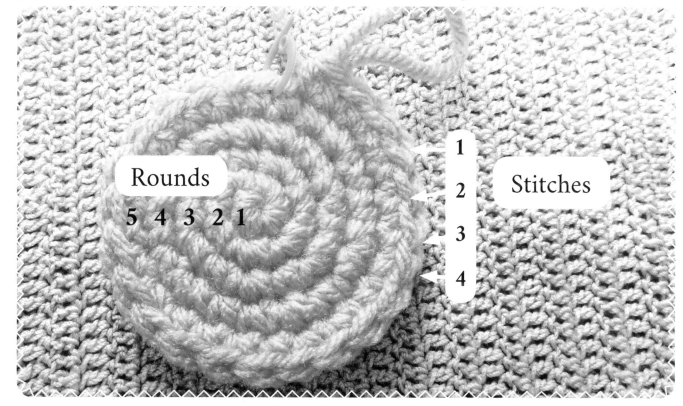

Rounds

5 4 3 2 1

1
2
3
4

Stitches

How to crochet the first round of the magic ring foundation

Rnd 1: 6 sc in a magic ring. (6 sc stitches made)

First make a magic ring (see previous page), yarn over, pull through loop on the hook.

Insert hook through the ring, yarn over,
pull through the ring.

You will have 2 loops on the hook.

Yarn over, pull through both loops on the hook.

One single crochet is made.

Repeat from (3) five times more, until 6 single crochet stitches made.

Pull the yarn end to close the ring.

6 sc in "a magic ring" is made.

Pull

27

Foundation Chain

Sometimes an Amigurumi doll is starting from chains and you will crochet the rows or rounds of your project on top of these chains. This will create an oval, square or rectangular shape.

How to crochet the first round around the foundation chain

Rnd 1: ch 12, sc in second chain from hook, sc in next 9 chs, 3 sc in next ch; working in remaining loops on opposite side of chain, sc in next 9 chs, 2 sc in next ch. **(24)**

The colors in the diagram below are the same colors as in the above instructions.

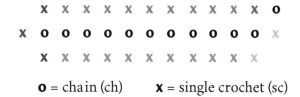

o = chain (ch)   **x** = single crochet (sc)

Make 12 chains.

Sc in second chain from hook.

Sc in next 9 chains.

3 sc in next chain.

Working in remaining loops on opposite side of chain, sc in next 9 chs,

2 sc in next chain. (24)

How to embroider the mouth for a Big Doll

The same embroidery technique can be used for the eyes of Ooble on page 54 and the large 8.3" Cushie doll on the opposite page.

How to embroider the mouth for a Small Doll

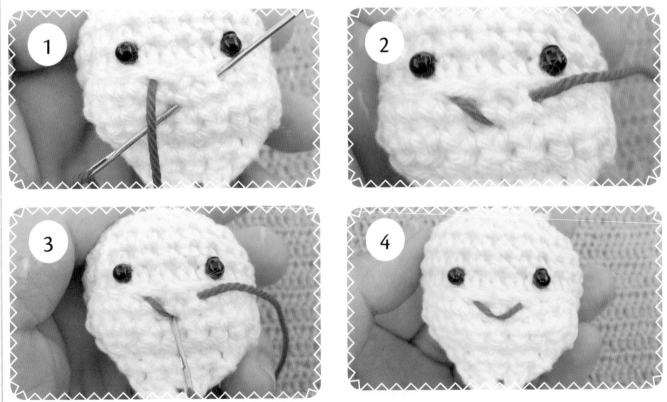

Gauge

Gauge is the number of stitches per inch and rows per inch that result from a specified yarn worked with a specified-size hook. Gauge is also done by individual tension. Tension is just how tight or loose you hold your yarn while you are crocheting. The measurements of individual work can vary greatly when using the same-size hook and yarn.

When making a doll, the gauge is not important. If your doll is a little bit bigger or smaller, it does not matter much. But if you are making a hat or sweater, the gauge is very important. If the gauge does not match the gauge given in the pattern, the item you are making will not end up the correct size.

Crochet Patterns

Doll Size

The size of the doll depends on the size of the crochet hook, the thickness of yarn and how you stuff it; a bigger hook and thicker yarn make a bigger doll. A doll stuffed tightly is bigger than a loose stuffed doll.

The picture below shows this : the smallest doll was made from one strand of DK yarn and a 3 mm hook, the medium sized doll was made from chunky yarn and a 4 mm hook and the biggest doll was made from crocheting 2 strands of DK yarn together with a 5 mm hook.

4.7" or 12 cm   7.3" or 18.5 cm   8.3" or 21 cm (excluding ears)

Abbreviations
US Crochet Abbreviations

ch = chain
sc = single crochet
st = stitch
sl = slip
rnd = round
tog = together

Remarks

The projects in this book are working in continuous rounds, do not join or turn unless otherwise stated. Mark first stitch of each round.

Bunnies

Materials

- For medium bunny:
  Chunky, Bulky yarn,
  brand : Stylecraft Special Chunky,
  color : Cloud Blue 1019 = 65 g
- a little bit of Black DK yarn to embroider
  the mouth (optional)
- 4.00 mm hook (US: G/6, UK: 8)
- Tapestry needle
- Polyester fiberfill = 60 g.
- One pair of 9 mm safety eyes
- Iron wire:12 inches long (30 cm), 18 gauge
  (1.25 mm thick)

Size

The blue, medium sized bunny is 10.3 inches tall
(26 cm).

Ear

Make 2.

Rnd 1: With **Cloud Blue 1019** and 4 mm hook,
6 sc in a magic ring. (6)
Rnd 2: (Sc in next st, 2 sc in next st) around. (9)
Rnd 3: (2 sc in next st, sc in next 2 sts) around. (12)
Rnd 4-10: Sc in each st around. (12)
Rnd 11: Sc next 2 sts tog, sc in next 10 sts. (11)
Rnd 12: Sc in each st around. (11)
Rnd 13: Sc in next 5 sts, sc next 2 sts tog,
sc in next 4 sts. (10)
Rnd 14: Sc in each st around. (10)
Rnd 15: Sc next 2 sts tog, sc in next 8 sts. (9)
Rnd 16: Sc in each st around. (9)
Rnd 17: Sc in next 4 sts, sc next 2 sts tog,
sc in next 3 sts. (8)
Rnd 18: Sc in each st around. (8)
Rnd 19: Sc next 2 sts tog, sc in next 6 sts. (7)

Rnd 20: Sc in each st around. (7)
Rnd 21: Sc in next 3 sts, sc next 2 sts tog, sc in next 2 sts. (6)
Rnd 22-23: Sc in each st around. (6)
Rnd 24: Sc in each st around. (6)

For the first ear, join with sl st in first st. Fasten off.
For the second ear, do not sl st in first st.
Do not fasten off.

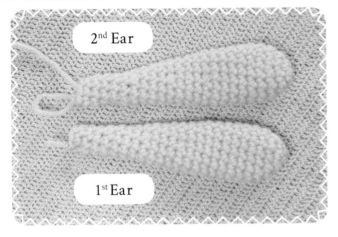

Body

The yarn of the second ear is used to start the body.
Rnd 1: Sc in the stitch on rnd 24 of the first ear (mark first st), sc in next 5 sts on first ear, sc in next 6 sts on second ear. (12)

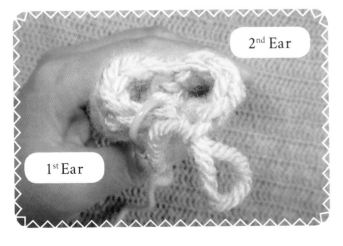

Rnd 2: (Sc in next st, 2 sc in next st) around. (18)
Rnd 3: Sc in each st around. (18)
Rnd 4: (2 sc in next st, sc in next 2 sts) around. (24)
Rnd 5: Sc in each st around. (24)
Rnd 6: (Sc in next 3 sts, 2 sc in next st) around. (30)
Rnd 7: Sc in each st around. (30)
Rnd 8: Sc in next 2 sts, 2 sc in next st, (sc in next 4 sts, 2 sc in next st) 5 times, sc in next 2 sts. (36)
Rnd 9: Sc in each st around. (36)
Rnd 10: (Sc in next 5 sts, 2 sc in next st) around. (42)
Rnd 11: Sc in each st around. (42)
Rnd 12: Sc in next 3 sts, 2 sc in next st, (sc in next 6 sts, 2 sc in next st) 5 times, sc in next 3 sts. (48)
Rnd 13: Sc in each st around. (48)
Rnd 14: (Sc in next 7 sts, 2 sc in next st) around. (54)
Rnd 15: Sc in each st around. (54)
Rnd 16: Sc in next 4 sts, 2 sc in next st, (sc in next 8 sts, 2 sc in next st) 5 times, sc in next 4 sts. (60)
Rnd 17-22: Sc in each st around. (60)
Rnd 23: Sc in next 4 sts, sc next 2 sts tog, (sc in next 8 sts, sc next 2 sts tog) 5 times, sc in next 4 sts. (54)
Rnd 24: (Sc in next 7 sts, sc next 2 sts tog) around. (48)
Rnd 25: Sc in next 3 sts, sc next 2 sts tog, (sc in next 6 sts, sc next 2 sts tog) 5 times, sc in next 3 sts. (42)
Rnd 26: (Sc in next 5 sts, sc next 2 sts tog) around. (36)
Rnd 27: Sc in next 2 sts, sc next 2 sts tog, (sc in next 4 sts, sc next 2 sts tog) 5 times, sc in next 2 sts, sl st in first st, fasten off. (30)

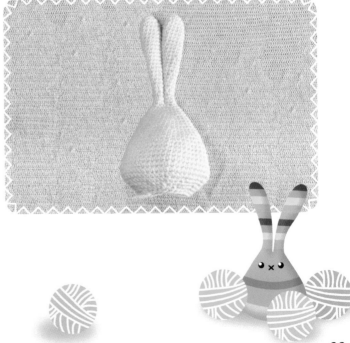

Bottom

With Chunky yarn and 4 mm hook.

Rnd 1: With Cloud Blue 1019,
6 sc in a magic ring. (6)
Rnd 2: 2 sc in each st around. (12)
Rnd 3: (Sc in next st, 2 sc in next st) around. (18)
Rnd 4: (2 sc in next st, sc in next 2 sts) around. (24)
Rnd 5: (Sc in next 3 sts, 2 sc in next st) around,
join with sl st in first st, leave long end for sewing,
fasten off. (30)

Finishing

Fold the wire in half and make it as long as the
ear by folding the ends of wire, see picture below.
Insert the wire inside ears.

Insert safety eyes 3 sts apart between rnds 27-28.

Do not stuff ears. Stuff body tightly then sew the
bottom piece to the last round of the body.

With Black DK yarn embroider a little x-cross
between the eyes on rnd 28.

♥ The smallest size Bunny is made with DMC Petra No.3 and a 3 mm hook.
♥ The medium size Bunny is made with Chunky yarn and a 4 mm hook.
♥ The biggest size Bunny is made by crocheting 4 strands of DK yarn together with a 6 mm hook.

34

Cushionette ♡

Materials

- ♥ Chunky, Bulky yarn,
  Brand : Stylecraft Special Chunky,
  color : White 1001 = 20 g
- ♥ DK, Light Worsted yarn,
  Stylecraft Special DK, color : a little bit
  of Black and Pink for eyes and mouth
- ♥ 4.00 mm hook (US: G/6, UK: 8)
- ♥ 3.00 mm hook (US: C/2 or D/3, UK: 11)
- ♥ Tapestry needle
- ♥ Pins
- ♥ Polyester fiberfill = 15 g.

Size

Cushionette is 4.1 inches tall (10.5 cm). This excludes
the ears.

Body

With Chunky yarn and 4 mm hook.

Rnd 1: With **White 1001** and 4 mm hook, ch 12,
sc in second chain from hook, sc in next 9 chs,
3 sc in next ch; working in remaining loops on
opposite side of chain, sc in next 9 chs,
2 sc in next ch. (24)

See diagram on page 28.

Rnd 2-15: Sc in each st around. (24)

Rnd 16: First leg, sc in next 6 sts, skip 16 sts, sc in next 2 sts. (8)

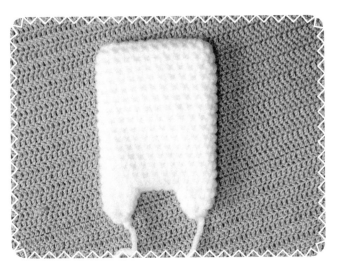

Sew the hole at the end of both feet closed.

Stuff the body and feet and sew the opening closed.

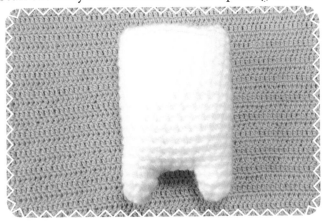

Rnd 17: Sc in each st around. (8)
Rnd 18: Sc next 2 sts tog around, join with sl st in first st, leave long end for sewing, fasten off. (4)

Rnd 16: Second leg, skip 4 sts from the first leg, join **White 1001** in the 5th st, ch 1, sc in same st, sc in next 7 sts. (8)

Ear

With Chunky yarn and 4 mm hook. Make 2.
With **White 1001** and 4 mm hook, ch 2, sc in second chain from hook; spikes : (ch 2, sl st in second ch from hook, sl st in the first sc) 3 times, leave long end for sewing, fasten off.

Rnd 17: Sc in each st around. (8)
Rnd 18: Sc next 2 sts tog around, join with sl st in first st, leave long end for sewing, fasten off. (4)

Pin ears on top and sew.

Arm

With Chunky yarn and 4 mm hook. Make 2.
Rnd 1: With **White 1001** and 4 mm hook,
6 sc in a magic ring. (6)
Rnd 2: Sc in each st around. (6)
Rnd 3: Sc in each st around, join with sl st in first st,
leave long end for sewing, fasten off. (6)

Do not stuff arms, pin arms to rnds 9-10 of the
body and sew.

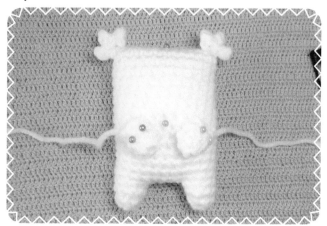

Eye

With DK yarn and 3 mm hook. Make 2.
Rnd 1: With **Black 1002** and 3 mm hook, ch 4,
sc in second chain from hook, sc in next ch, 3 sc in
next ch; working in remaining loops on opposite side
of chain, sc in next ch, 2 sc in next ch, sl st in first st,
leave long end for sewing, fasten off. (8)

```
    x  x  x  o        x = single crochet (sc)
 x  o  o  o  x
    x  x  x           o = chain (ch)
```

With **White** DK yarn embroider a cross on the
black eyes.

Sew eyes over rnds 4-6 from the top.

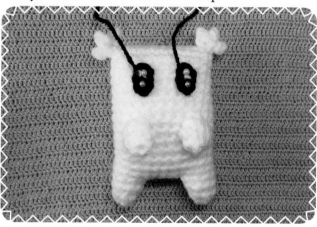

Mouth

With **Pink** DK yarn (Fondant 1241)
embroider the mouth.

Chickalee

Materials

- Chunky, Bulky yarn, brand : Stylecraft Special Chunky, color : Meado 1065 = 40 g
- DK, Light Worsted, Stylecraft Special DK, color : a little bit of Citron 1263, Fiesta 1257, Violet 1277, Turquoise 1068, Jaffa 1256, White 1001 and Black 1002
- 3.00 mm hook (US: C/2 or D/3, UK: 11)
- 4.00 mm hook (US: G/6, UK: 8)
- Tapestry needle
- Pins
- Polyester fiberfill = 25 g
- Plastic Pellets = 4 oz (120 g)
- A small piece of stocking for containing the plastic pellets

Size

From bottom to top of comb: 4.5 inch (11.5 cm)
Length from head to tail: 8 inch (20 cm)

Tail

With DK yarn and 3 mm hook, make one each in Fiesta 1257, Violet 1277, Turquoise 1068.

Rnd 1: With Fiesta 1257 (pink) and 3 mm hook, 6 sc in a magic ring. (6)
Rnd 2: Sc in each st around. (6)
Rnd 3: (Sc in next st, 2 sc in next st) around. (9)
Rnd 4-7: Sc in each st around. (9)
Rnd 8: (Sc next 2 sts tog, sc in next st) around. (6)
Rnd 9: Sc in each st around. (6)
Rnd 10: Sc next 2 sts tog around. (3)
Rnd 11: Sc in each st around, sl st in first st, fasten off. (3)

Sew 3 pieces of tail together.

Body & Head

With Chunky yarn and 4 mm hook.
Rnd 1: Body, with **Meadow1065**,
6 sc in a magic ring. (6)
Rnd 2: 2 sc in each st around. (12)
Rnd 3: (2 sc in next st, sc in next st) around. (18)
Rnd 4: (Sc in next 2 sts, 2 sc in next st) around. (24)
Rnd 5: (Sc in next 3 sts, 2 sc in next st) around. (30)
Rnd 6: Sc in next 2 sts, 2 sc in next st, (sc in next 4 sts, 2 sc in next st) 5 times, sc in next 2 sts. (36)
Rnd 7: (Sc in next 5 sts, 2 sc in next st) around. (42)
Rnd 8: Sc in next 3 sts, 2 sc in next st, (sc in next 6 sts, 2 sc in next st) 5 times, sc in next 3 sts. (48)
Rnd 9-16: Sc in each st around. (48)
Rnd 17: Head, 2 sc in next 9 sts. (18)

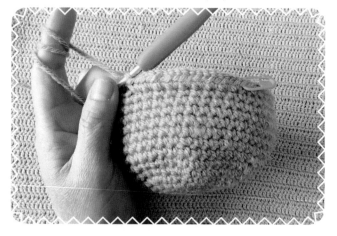

Rnd 18: 2 sc in each st around. (36)
The pictures below show the first 2 stitches of rnd 18.

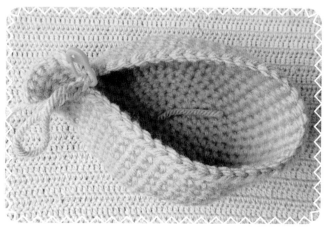

Rnd 19-25: Sc in each st around. (36)
Rnd 26: (Sc in next 4 sts, sc next 2 sts tog) around. (30)
Rnd 27: Sc in each st around. (30)
Rnd 28: (Sc in next 3 sts, sc next 2 sts tog) around. (24)
Rnd 29: (Sc in next 2 sts, sc next 2 sts tog) around. (18)
Rnd 30: (Sc in next st, sc next 2 sts tog) around. (12)
Rnd 31: Sc next 2 sts tog around, sl st in first st, fasten off. (6)

Stuff head with polyester fiberfill.

Sew the opening closed but leave 1-1.5 cm at the end to put the tail in.

Fill stocking with plastic Pellets then tie the knot.

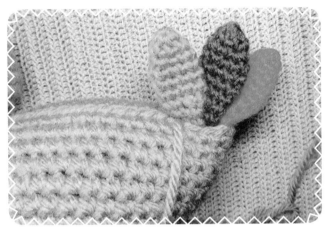

Put the filled stocking inside the body.

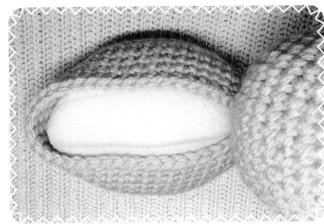

Sew the opening closed.

Wing

With DK yarn and 3 mm hook, make 2.

Rnd 1: With **Bright Orange 981** and 3 mm hook, 6 sc in a magic ring. (6)

Rnd 2: 2 sc in each st around. (12)

Rnd 3-5: Sc in each st around. (12)

Rnd 6: 2 sc in next st, sc in next 10 sts, 2 sc in next st. (14)

Rnd 7-8: Sc in each st around. (14)

Rnd 9: Sl st in next st, 4 sc in next st, sl st in next st, 4 sc in next st, sl st in next st, 4 sc in next st, sl st in next 2 sts, 4 sc in next st, sl st in next st, 4 sc in next st, sl st in next st, 4 sc in next st, sl st in next st, leave long end for sewing, fasten off.

("4 sc in next st" is working 4 sc in the same st.)

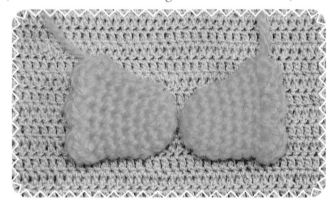

Use pins to position wings on both sides of the body and sew.

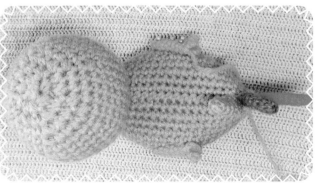

Comb

With DK yarn and 3 mm hook, make 4.

Rnd 1: With **Jaffa 1256** and 3 mm hook, 6 sc in a magic ring.

Rnd 2: Sc in each st around. (6)

Rnd 3: (Sc in next st, 2 sc in next st) around. (9)

Rnd 4: Sc in each st around. (9)

Rnd 5: Sc in each st around, sl st in first st, leave long end for sewing, fasten off.

Pin comb on top of head and sew.

Eye

Make the same as Cushionette's Eye pattern.
See page 37.
Pin eyes on head and sew.

Mouth

With DK yarn color Citron 1263: embroider the mouth.

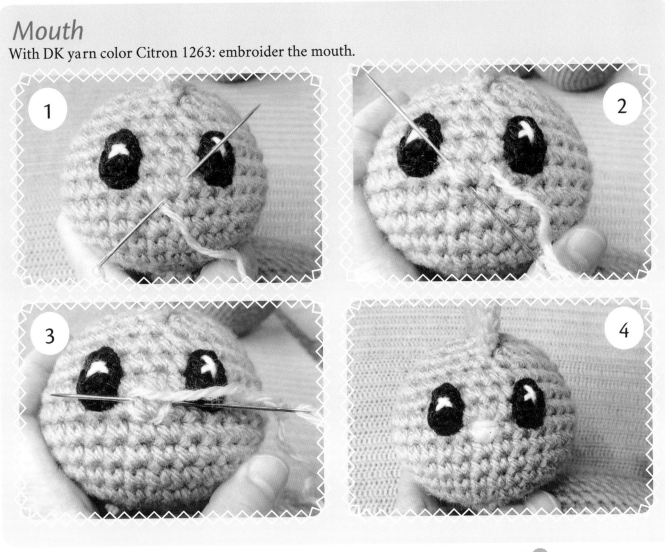

Cushie

Materials

- Chunky, Bulky yarn,
  brand: Stylecraft Special Baby Chunky,
  color: Baby Pink 1230 = 60 g
- DK, Light Worsted,
  Stylecraft Special DK, colors: a little bit
  of Black 1002 and White 1001
- 3.00 mm hook (US: C/2 or D/3, UK: 11)
- 4.00 mm hook (US: G/6, UK: 8)
- Pink Embroidery Thread or Pink DK yarn
  (Fondant 1241) to embroider the mouth
- Tapestry needle
- Pins
- Polyester fiberfill = 40 g.

Size

On page 30 is a photo of the different doll sizes.
The Chunky yarn and a 4 mm hook create a medium
sized doll, which is 7.3 inches or 18.5 cm tall.
43 (7.3" without the ears.)

Body

With Chunky yarn and 4 mm hook.

Rnd 1: With **Baby Pink 1230** and 4 mm hook, ch 22,
sc in second chain from hook, sc in next 19 chs, 3 sc
in next ch; working in remaining loops on opposite
side of chain, sc in next 19 chs, 2 sc in next ch. (44)

x	x	x	x	x	....		x	x	x	o
x	o	o	o	o	o	....		o	o	o	x
x	x	x	x		....			x	x	x	

o = chain (ch)   x = single crochet (sc)

Rnd 2-29: Sc in each st around. (44)

Rnd 30: First leg, sc in next 11 sts, skip 30 sts, sc in next 3 sts. (14)

Rnd 31-34: Sc in each st around. (14)
Rnd 35: Sc next 2 sts tog around, join with sl st in first st, leave long end for sewing, fasten off. (7)

Rnd 30: Second leg, skip 8 sts from the first leg, join **Baby Pink 1230** in the 9th st, ch 1, sc in same st, sc in next 13 sts. (14)

Rnd 31-34: Sc in each st around. (14)
Rnd 35: Sc next 2 sts tog around, join with sl st in first st, leave long end for sewing, fasten off. (7)

Sew the hole at the end of both feet closed.
Stuff the body and feet and sew the opening closed.

Arm

With Chunky yarn and 4 mm hook, make 2.
Rnd 1: With **Baby Pink 1230** and 4 mm hook, 6 sc in a magic ring. (6)
Rnd 2: (Sc in next st, 2 sc in next st) around. (9)
Rnd 3-6: Sc in each st around. (9)
Rnd 7: Sc in each st around, join with sl st in first st, leave long end for sewing, fasten off. (9)

Stuff arms a little bit and sew the opening closed flat.

Pin arms to rnds 18-20 of the body and sew.

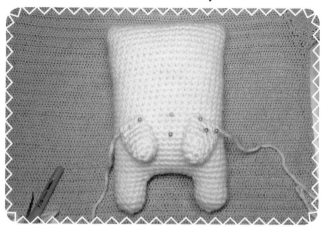

Ear

With Chunky yarn and 4 mm hook, make 2.

With **Baby Pink 1230** and 4 mm hook, ch 2, sc in second ch from hook; spikes: (ch 5, sl st in second ch from hook, sl st in next 3 chs, sl st in the first sc) 3 times, leave long end for sewing, fasten off.

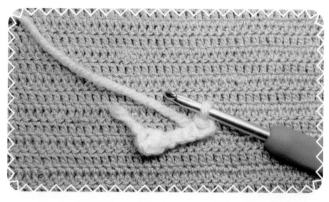

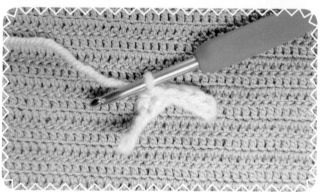

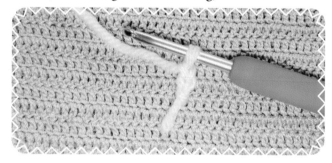

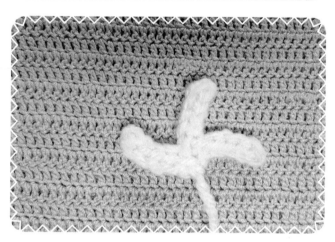

Pin ears on top and sew.

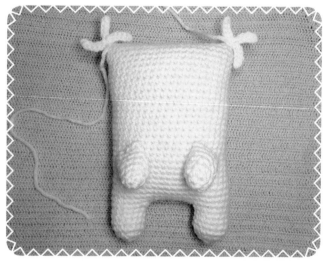

Eye
With DK yarn and 3 mm hook.

White Eye
Make 2.

Rnd 1: With **White 1001** and 3 mm hook, 5 sc in a magic ring, sl st in first st, leave long end for sewing, fasten off. (5)

Black Eye
Make 2.

Rnd 1: With **Black 1002** and 3 mm hook, ch 5, sc in second chain from hook, sc in next 2 chs, 3 sc in next ch; working in remaining loops on opposite side of chain, sc in next 2 chs, 2 sc in next ch. (10)

```
    x  x  x  x  o
  x  o  o  o  o  x
    x  x  x  x
```

o = chain (ch)   x = single crochet (sc)

Rnd 2: 2 sc in next st, sc in next 2 sts, 2 sc in next 3 sts, sc in next 2 sts, 2 sc in next 2 sts, sl st in first st, leave long end for sewing, fasten off. (16)

Sew white eye on top of the black eye.

Sew eyes on rnds 7-11 from the top.

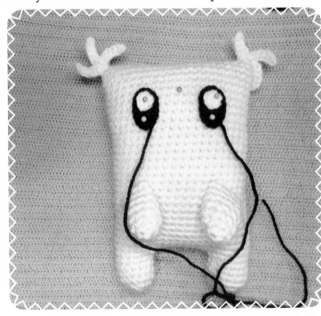

Mouth

Use pins to mark the mouth line.

With DK yarn color **Pink** (Fondant 1241) embroider the mouth.

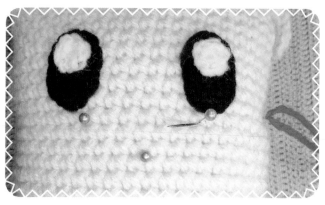

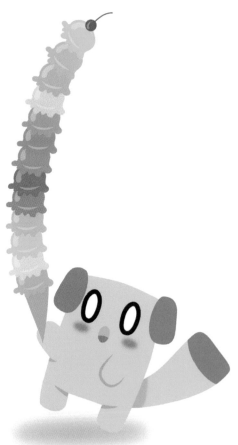

Jinco ♡

Materials

5 Bulky

- ❤ Chunky, Bulky yarn,
  Stylecraft Special Chunky, colors :
  Fondant 1241 = 80 g, Raspberry 1023 = 15 g
- ❤ DK, Light Worsted,
  Stylecraft Special DK : a little bit of **3 Light**
  Black 1002 and White 1001
- ❤ 3.00 mm hook (US: C/2 or D/3, UK: 11)
- ❤ 4.00 mm hook (US: G/6, UK: 8)
- ❤ Tapestry needle
- ❤ Pins
- ❤ Polyester fiberfill = 60 g.

Size

Jinco is 7 inches tall. (17.5 cm)

Body

With Chunky yarn and 4 mm hook.

Rnd 1: With **Fondant 1241** and 4 mm hook, ch 24, sc in second chain from hook, sc in next 21 chs, 3 sc in next ch, sc in next 21 chs, 2 sc in next ch. (48)

	x	x	x	x	x	....		x	x	x	o
x	o	o	o	o	o	....		o	o	o	x
	x	x	x	x	x	....		x	x	x	

o = chain (ch)   x = single crochet (sc)

Rnd 2-25: Sc in each st around. (48)

Rnd 26: First leg, sc in next 10 sts, skip 34 sts, sc in next 4 sts. (14)

Rnd 27-29: Sc in each st around. (14)

Rnd 30: Sc next 2 sts tog around, join with sl st in first st, leave long end for sewing, fasten off. (7)

Rnd 26: Second leg, skip 10 sts from the first leg, join **Fondant 1241** in the 11ᵗʰ st, ch 1, sc in same st, sc in next 13 sts. (14)

Rnd 27-29: Sc in each st around. (14)

Rnd 30: Sc next 2 sts tog around, join with sl st in first st, leave long end for sewing, fasten off. (7)

Sew the hole at the end of both feet closed.

Stuff the body and feet and sew the opening closed.

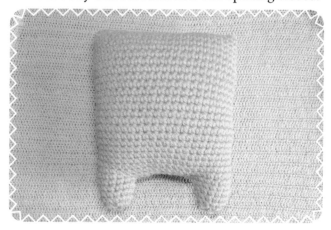

Ear

With Chunky yarn and 4 mm hook, make 2.

Rnd 1: With **Raspberry 1023** and 4 mm hook, ch 5, sc in second chain from hook, sc in next 2 chs, 3 sc in next ch, sc in next 2 chs, 2 sc in next ch. (10)

```
        x  x  x  x  o
     x  o  o  o  o  x
        x  x  x  x
```

o = chain (ch)   x = single crochet (sc)

Rnd 2-6: Sc in each st around. (10)

Rnd 7: Sc next 2 sts tog, sc in next 3 sts, sc next 2 sts tog, sc in next 3 sts, join with sl st in first st, leave long end for sewing, fasten off. (8)

Pin ears on top and sew.

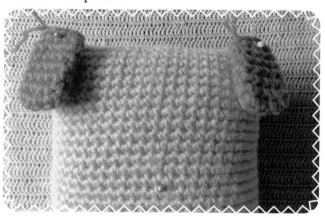

Arm

Same as Cushie's arm pattern, use **Fondant 1241**, see page 44.

Pin arms on rnds 16-18 of the body and sew.

Eye

Same as Cushie's eye pattern, see page 46.

Pin eyes on rnds 7-10 of the body and sew.

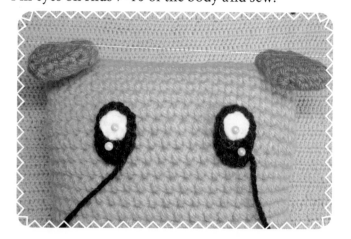

Tail

With Chunky yarn and 4 mm hook.

Rnd 1: With **Raspberry 1023** and 4 mm hook, ch 10, sc in second chain from hook, sc in next 7 chs, 3 sc in next ch, sc in next 7 chs, 2 sc in next ch. (20)

o = chain (ch)   x = single crochet (sc)

Rnd 2-3: Sc in each st around. (20)

Rnd 4: Sc in each st around, changing to **Fondant 1241** in last 2 loops of last st. (20)

Rnd 5: Sc in each st around. (20)

Rnd 6: (Sc next 2 sts tog, sc in next 8 sts) 2 times. (18)

Rnd 7-8: Sc in each st around. (18)

Rnd 9: (Sc next 2 sts tog, sc in next 7 sts) 2 times. (16)

Rnd 10-11: Sc in each st around. (16)

Rnd 12: (Sc next 2 sts tog, sc in next 6 sts) 2 times. (14)

Rnd 13-17: Sc in each st around. (14)

Rnd 18: (Sc next 2 sts tog, sc in next 5 sts) 2 times. (12)

Rnd 19-24: Sc in each st around. (12)

Rnd 25: Sc in each st around, join with sl st in first st, leave long end for sewing, fasten off. (12)

Stuff tail a little bit and sew the opening closed flat.

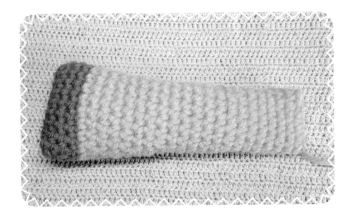

Pin tail on rnd 18-22 of the body and sew the last 3 rnds of the tail to the body.

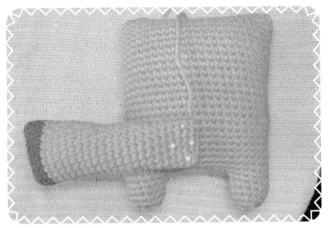

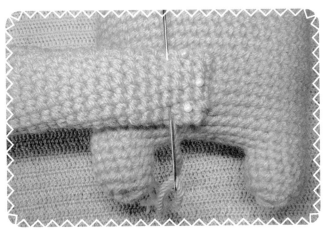

Ooble ♥

Materials

- ♥ Chunky, Bulky,
  brand : Stylecraft Special Chunky,
  color : Graphite 1063 = 80 g
- ♥ DK, Light Worsted yarn,
  brand : Stylecraft Special DK,
  colors : a little bit of White 1001, Citron 1263,
  Graphite 1063 and Black 1002
- ♥ 3.00 mm hook (US: C/2 or D/3, UK: 11)
- ♥ 4.00 mm hook (US: G/6, UK: 8)
- ♥ Tapestry needle
- ♥ Pins
- ♥ Polyester fiberfill = 50 g.

Size

Ooble is 7.9 inch tall without the ears. (20 cm)

Body

Same as Cushie's body pattern, use color **Graphite 1063,** see page 43.

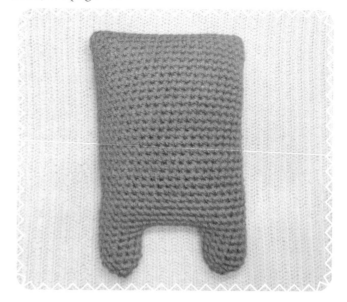

Arm

Same as Cushie's arm pattern, use **Graphite 1063**, see page 44.

Stuff arm a little bit, sew the opening closed flat.

Pin arms on rnds 20-23 of the body and sew.

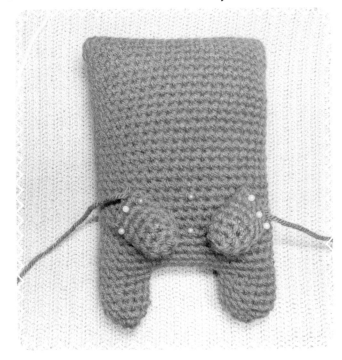

Ear

With Chunky yarn and 4 mm hook, make 2.

Rnd 1: With **Graphite 1063** and 4 mm hook, 4 sc in a magic ring. (4)

Rnd 2: 2 sc in next st, sc in next 3 sts. (5)

Rnd 3: Sc in next 2 sts, 2 sc in next st, sc in next 2 sts. (6)

Rnd 4: (Sc in next st, 2 sc in next st) around. (9)

Rnd 5-6: Sc in each st around. (9)

Rnd 7: (Sc in next 2 sts, 2 sc in next st) around. (12)

Rnd 8-9: Sc in each st around. (12)

Rnd 10: (Sc in next 3 sts, 2 sc in next st) around. (15)

Rnd 11: Sc in each st around. (15)

Rnd 12: Sc in each st around, join with sl st in first st, leave long end for sewing, fasten off. (15)

Do not stuff ears, pin ears on top and sew.

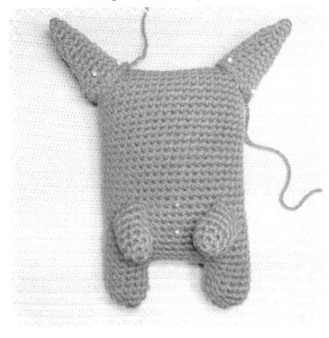

Tie

With DK yarn and 3 mm hook

Rnd 1: With **Citron 1263** and 3 mm hook, 6 sc in a magic ring. (6)

Rnd 2: Sc in each st around. (6)

Rnd 3: 2 sc in each st around. (12)

Rnd 4: (Sc next 2 sts tog, sc in next 2 sts) around. (9)

Rnd 5-7: Sc in each st around. (9)

Rnd 8: Sc next 2 sts tog, sc in next 7 sts. (8)

Rnd 9: Sc in each st around. (8)

Rnd 10: Sc next 2 sts tog, sc in next 6 sts. (7)

Rnd 11: Sc next 2 sts tog, sc in next 5 sts. (6)

Rnd 12: Sc in each st around. (6)

Rnd 13: Sc in each st around, join with sl st in next st, leave long end for sewing , fasten off.

Pin tie on rnd 17 of body and sew.

Collar

With DK yarn and 3 mm hook

Row 1: With **White 1001** and 3 mm hook, ch 70, sc in second chain from hook, sc in next 68 chs, turn. (69)

Row 2: Ch 1, 2 sc in first st, sc in next 67 sts, 2 sc in next st, leave long end for sewing, fasten off. (71)

Put collar around body and pin both ends on top of the tie.

On the back of the Ooble doll: pin collar on rnd 13 of the body. Sew collar to the body.

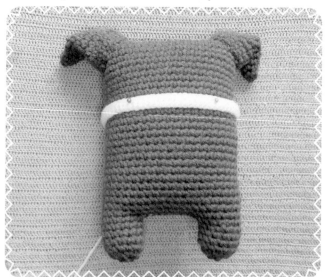

Snout
With DK yarn and 3 mm hook

Rnd 1: With **Black 1002** and 3 mm hook, 6 sc in a magic ring, changing to **Graphite 1063** in last 2 loops of last st. (6)

Rnd 2: <u>Working in back loops only</u>. Sc in each st around. (6)

Rnd 3: 2 sc in next 3 sts, sc in next 3 sts. (9)

Rnd 4: Sc in each st around. (9)

Rnd 5: Sc in next 2 sts, 2 sc in next 3 sts, sc in next 4 sts. (12)

Rnd 6: Sc in each st around. (12)

Rnd 7: Sc in next 4 sts, 2 sc in next 3 sts, sc in next 5 sts, join with sl st in first st, leave long end for sewing, fasten off. (15)

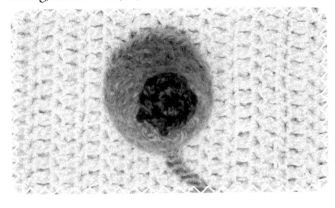

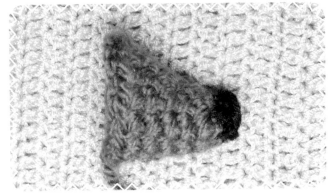

Stuff snout, pin it on rnds 11-14 of body and sew.

Eye
With **Black 1002** embroider the eye lines. I used pins to mark the eye lines. See how to embroider the eye lines on page 29 (same as mouth).

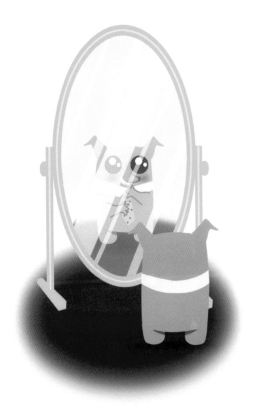

54

Inky ♡

Materials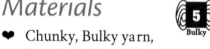

- ♥ Chunky, Bulky yarn,
  brand : Stylecraft Special Chunky,
  colors : Midnight 1011 = 60 g, a little bit of
  Black 1002 and White 1001
- ♥ DK, Light Worsted,
  Stylecraft Special DK, colors: a little bit
  of Gold 1709, White 1001 and Black 1002
- ♥ 3.00 mm hook (US: C/2 or D/3, UK: 11)
- ♥ 4.00 mm hook (US: G/6, UK: 8)
- ♥ Tapestry needle
- ♥ Pins
- ♥ Polyester fiberfill = 60 g.

Size

Inky is 5.9 inches tall including the hat. (15 cm)

Tentacle

With Chunky yarn and 4 mm hook, make 7.

Rnd 1: With **Midnight 1011** and 4 mm hook,
6 sc in a magic ring. (6)

Rnd 2-3: Sc in each st around. (6)

Rnd 4: Sc next 2 sts tog, sc in next st,
2 sc in next 2 sts, sc in next st. (7)

Rnd 5: Sc next 2 sts tog, sc in next 2 sts,
2 sc in next st, sc in next 2 sts. (7)

Rnd 6: Sc in each st around.

Rnd 7: Sc next 2 sts tog, sc in next st,
2 sc in next 3 sts, sc in next st. (9)

Rnd 8: Sc next 2 sts tog, sc in next 2 sts,
2 sc in next 3 sts, sc in next 2 sts,
join with sl st in first st, leave long end
for sewing, fasten off. (11)

Finished tentacle:

Sew the tentacles around the base.

Do not stuff tentacles, sew the opening close flat.

Base

With Chunky yarn and 4 mm hook.

Rnd 1: With **Midnight 1011** and 4 mm hook,
6 sc in a magic ring. (6)

Rnd 2: 2 sc in each st around. (12)

Rnd 3: (2 sc in next st, sc in next st) around. (18)

Rnd 4: (Sc in next 2 sts, 2 sc in next st) around. (24)

Rnd 5: (Sc in next 3 sts, 2 sc in next st) around,
sl st in first st, fasten off. (30)

Rnd 7: Sc in each st around. (36)
Rnd 8: (Sc in next 5 sts, 2 sc in next st) around. (42)
Rnd 9: Sc in next 3 sts, 2 sc in next st, (sc in next 6 sts, 2 sc in next st) 5 times, sc in next 3 sts. (48)
Rnd 10-16: Sc in each st around. (48)
Rnd 17: (Sc in next 6 sts, sc next 2 sts tog) around. (42)
Rnd 18: Sc in each st around. (42)
Rnd 19: (Sc in next 5 sts, sc next 2 sts tog) around. (36)
Rnd 20: (Sc in next 4 sts, sc next 2 sts tog) around. (30)
Rnd 21-23: Sc in each st around. (30)
Rnd 24: Sc in each st around, join with sl st in first st, fasten off. (30)

Stuff the body and sew the base to the bottom of the body.

Body

With Chunky yarn and a 4 mm hook.

Rnd 1: With **Midnight 1011**, 6 sc in a magic ring. (6)
Rnd 2: 2 sc in each st around. (12)
Rnd 3: (2 sc in next st, sc in next st) around. (18)
Rnd 4: (Sc in next 2 sts, 2 sc in next st) around. (24)
Rnd 5: (Sc in next 3 sts, 2 sc in next st) around. (30)
Rnd 6: Sc in next 2 sts, 2 sc in next st, (sc in next 4 sts, 2 sc in next st) 5 times, sc in next 2 sts. (36)

Eye

Make eyes the same as Cushie's, see page 46.
Sew eyes on rnds 9-13.

Stuff hat a little bit, then sew it on top of the body.

Hat

Rnd 1: With **White 1001** and 4 mm hook,
6 sc in a magic ring. (6)
Rnd 2: 2 sc in each st around. (12)
Rnd 3: (2 sc in next st, sc in next st) around. (18)
Rnd 4: (Sc in next 2 sts, 2 sc in next st) around. (24)
Rnd 5: (Sc in next 3 sts, 2 sc in next st) around. (30)
Rnd 6: <u>Working in back loops only.</u>
Sc in each st around. (30)
Rnd 7: (Sc next 2 sts tog, sc in next st) around,
changing to **Black 1002** in last 2 loops of last st. (20)
Rnd 8: Sc in each st around. (20)
Rnd 9: Sl st in each st around, leave long end
for sewing, fasten off.

Mouth

With Black DK yarn embroider mouth, see how to
embroider the mouth on page 29.

58

2 sc in next st, turn. (9)
Row 5: Ch 1, 2 sc in first st, sc in next 7 sts, 2 sc in next st, turn. (11)
Row 6: Ch 1, 2 sc in first st, sc in next 9 sts, 2 sc in next st, fasten off. (13)

Part 2

Row 1: With **Gold 1709** and 3 mm hook, ch 50; working on the last row of Part I, 2 sc in next st, sc in next 11 sts, 2 sc in next st, ch 20, turn. (ch 50, 15 sc, ch 20)

Scarf

With DK yarn and 3 mm hook

Part I

Row 1: With **Gold 1709** and 3 mm hook, ch 2, 3 sc in second chain from hook, turn. (3)
Row 2: Ch 1, 2 sc in first st, sc in next st, 2 sc in next st, turn. (5)
Row 3: Ch 1, 2 sc in first st, sc in next 3 sts, 2 sc in next st, turn. (7)
Row 4: Ch 1, 2 sc in first st, sc in next 5 sts,

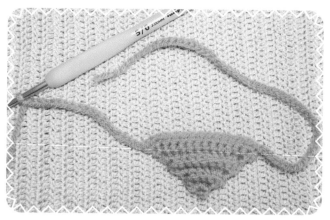

Row 2: Ch 1, sc in second chain from hook, sc in next 18 chs, working in back loops only; 2 sc in next st, sc in next 13 sts, 2 sc in next st, sc in next 50 chs, fasten off.

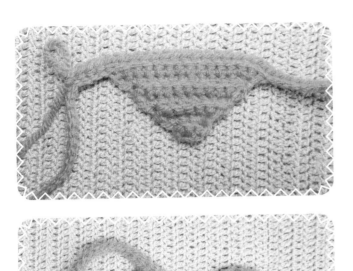

Put scarf on Inky.

60

From the Authors

Cushie and Cushionette came out of the pencil of Jasmine Appelboom. She invented their character and looks. Soon they were joined by other characters and lived many adventures, which she'd share with her brother. Jasmine's mother, Sayjai crocheted the dolls and added the patterns to the book. Maria was so kind to turn Jasmine's sketches into beautiful illustrations. Rob helped with editing.
A lot of work went into this book. We hope you'll love it as much as we do.

Jasmine, Sayjai, Rob and Maria

Copyright

First Edition, Publication date: 16th of July 2017
Publisher: K and J Publishing, 16 Whitegate Close, Swavesey Cambridge, CB24 4TT, England
For information on licensing, where to buy or questions about the patterns, please e-mail: kandjdolls@gmail.com.

Other pattern books written by Sayjai:

Huggy Dolls 2
Amigurumi Crochet Patterns

Publication date: 15th of April 2016
ISBN: 978-1910407417

Huggy Dolls Amigurumi
15 Huggable Doll Patterns

Publication date: 14th of June 2014
ISBN: 978-1910407028

Easy Amigurumi
28 doll patterns

Publication date: 18th of July 2014
ISBN: 978-1910407011

Dress Up Dolls Amigurumi
5 big dolls with clothes, shoes, accessories, tiny bear and big carry bag patterns

Publication date: September 27th 2014
ISBN: 978-1910407066

Sunny Amigurumi
Crochet Patterns

Publication date: February 25th 2015
ISBN: 978-1910407189

Kawaii Amigurumi
28 Cute Animal Crochet Patterns

Publication date: June 27th 2015
ISBN: 978-1910407264

Christmas Amigurumi
Crochet Patterns

Publication date: November 19th 2015
ISBN: 978-1910407318